F A C E T  B O O K S

HISTORICAL SERIES — 20
(Medieval)

Heiko A. Oberman, Editor

The Virgin Mary
in Evangelical
Perspective

by HEIKO A. OBERMAN

with an Introduction by Thomas F. O'Meara, O.P.

FORTRESS PRESS   PHILADELPHIA

This study was first published in the *Journal of Ecumenical Studies* 1 (1964): 271–298, and is republished by arrangement with the author and the publisher.

Published by Fortress Press, 1971

Library of Congress Catalog Card Number 70–157546
ISBN 0–8006–3067–x

1926B71   Printed in U.S.A.   1-3067

Introduction

AMERICAN ecumenism is related to the rapid increase in the rate of change in all of contemporary American society. Over the past ten years, the advent and presence of the ecumenical movement in the United States has achieved a great deal: ecumenism is widely taken for granted, a considerable degree of cooperation has been reached in seminary and religious education, practical work on the social and ministerial levels is widespread. And, in at least some areas of the United States, there is an increased openness on the local level for real ecumenical contact between churches and parishes. But to this ecumenism has been counterpoised a deeper "ecumenical problem." The new crisis for the churches does not come from within their own structures or from their century-long conflicts with each other. It is the crisis of the world over against the church. It is the recognition that the world's turmoil, problems, and potentialities demand that the church really be the church. Christian churches are now challenged to go beyond interconfessional problems.

The result of all of this ecumenical and postecumenical activity in the United States has been to create a deep ecumenical atmosphere. Slowly but surely we have come to see that there are not many problems dividing the churches, but only a few. These remaining fundamental ecumenical problems are indeed serious. But they cannot be divorced from the problems which all of the churches together face in confronting contemporary American society. Among these remaining basic questions, those of grace and authority must certainly be included. For one thing, authority is being challenged at every level, and past uncomplicated assumptions of where the authority of Christian revelation lies now seem too simple. Second, in a personalistic and political society, the question as to what it means to be a Christian must be asked anew. Both of these questions are related to the men and women around Jesus Christ, especially Mary.

Dr. Heiko Oberman's study is an exposition of the problem of Mary by an intelligent and open European Protestant theologian. It is, generally, free from the past clichés and prejudices which have colored this topic of Mary within the context of Christianity. (One exception to this might be his retention of historical analogies, not looked at critically enough in terms of time and culture. These analogies link too facilely the role of woman in pagan religions and the development of devotion to the mother of Jesus Christ.) Dr. Oberman rightly emphasizes the biblical dimension, for it is the biblical word which for Protestants seems to say "no" to the apparent "creations" of Catholic devotion and theology. It is also the biblical word, understood from another hermeneutical point of view, which allows Catholicism to try to understand the text in a wider theological and devotional context. For example, different traditions evaluate Mary's presence among the first disciples in various ways. Dr. Oberman also offers the inescapable foundation for any Christian's attitude towards biblical persons other than Jesus Christ, namely, the Communion of Saints. The Pauline Mystical Body of Christ and the age-old Communion of Saints are the right context for every attitude towards the mother of Christ, towards the apostles, etc. As we will see at greater length below, Vatican II has reintroduced this context, placing Mary *within* the Church and not above or over it. This is the fundamental perspective of anything to be said about her. Finally, Dr. Oberman rightly points out, along with many other

authors, the interesting ambiguity in the thought of the Reformers themselves, especially Luther.

Most theologians in treating the problem of the Virgin Mary
are now able to go beyond the previous centuries of contro-
versies and debating points. They see that Mary is a point of
focus for the two or three crucial problems which remain and
which represent a different theological stance by Protestants and
Catholics. This is the thesis of my book, *Mary in Protestant and
Catholic Theology.*[1] It is developed at great length by Karl
Barth who writes:

> Marian dogma is neither more nor less than the critical, central
> dogma of the Roman Catholic Church, the dogma from the stand-
> point of which all their important positions are to be regarded and
> by which they stand or fall. . . . In the doctrine and worship of
> Mary there is disclosed the one heresy of the Roman Catholic Church
> which explains all the rest. The "mother of God" of Roman Cath-
> olic Marian dogma is quite simply the principle, type and essence
> of the human creature co-operating servantlike in its own redemption
> on the basis of prevenient grace, and to that extent the principle,
> type and essence of the Church.[2]

Dr. K. E. Skydsgaard has also seen the union of the basic
ecumenical problems in the figure of Mary.

> There is probably no place where the difference between the two
> understandings of Christianity becomes so plain as in their differing
> conceptions of the Virgin Mary. Evangelical theology knows that this
> teaching point . . . has often been distorted, and knows that it has a
> duty to clarify the Roman insights on this point as authentically and
> as reliably as possible. But as Evangelical theology gains insight into
> the Roman view of this question, and sees how completely pene-
> trating the role of Mariology is and how intimately it is knit into
> the deepest motives in Roman Catholicism, it grows in understanding
> how different the Evangelical and the Roman Catholic traditions are.[3]

Neither Skydsgaard nor Barth wants to imply that there
should be or necessarily must be a great deal of discussion about
Mary; they are not interested in conferences and journals about

1. Thomas O'Meara, O. P., *Mary in Protestant and Catholic Theology* (New
York: Sheed & Ward, 1966). The volume contains an extensive bibliography.
2. Karl Barth, *Church Dogmatics* (Edinburgh: T. and T. Clark, 1956), I/2,
143.
3. K. Skydsgaard, *One in Christ* (Philadelphia: Fortress, 1957), p. 207.

"Marian Theology." What they are pointing out (and what is the general thesis of my study) is that fundamental ecumenical problems merge together and are seen clearly in the doctrine of the mother of Christ. These questions are: (a) the problem of Scripture being the source of our knowledge about what happened and is happening in salvation-history; (b) the role of authority and of the development of theology within the Christian community; (c) the correct appreciation of justification, grace (in its many different aspects), and the Christian life. If we look briefly at each of these, we see how this is true.

(a) First of all, the primary source of witnessed revelation, as a record of our faith, must be the New Testament. The Protestant Reformation spoke of *sola scriptura* and recent Catholic theologians influential at Vatican II have emphasized that, in some way, all of our knowledge of revelation must be found in the Scriptures. Yet as Protestants point out, dogmas such as the Assumption and the Immaculate Conception, are not apparent in Scripture. The Protestant biblical mentality also has a tradition of interpreting certain ambiguous passages in a different light, raising the question of whether Mary doubted her son and as to whether she had children other than Jesus. The problem of interpreting Scripture is an enormous one. But here we should recognize immediately that both Protestants and Catholics in recent decades have modified what long appeared to be their "classic position." Catholics have spoken of the "contentual sufficiency" of the Scriptures, while Protestants through the radical work of form critics such as Rudolf Bultmann have been forced to the realization that the Scriptures themselves represent theological interpretations of the community, that there can be no creation or interpretation of the Scriptures apart from the living community—past and present —the Church.

(b) Differences in theology inevitably raise the problem of authority. What is the real authority of Scripture now that we see its intimate involvement in the early communities' different theologies? Karl Barth rightly noticed the ambiguous temporal connection of the statement of papal infallibility in 1870, and its relationship, lying between them as it did, to the two Marian dogmas of 1854 and 1950. There seemed to be a circle here. Protestantism naturally fears that such a strong ecclesiastical authority, apparently dominating even the Scriptures, could fashion belief in dogmas independent of the Word of God. On the other hand, Catholics, after Vatican II, are showing how the role of bishop and pope is involved in the wider context of the Church. Whatever charisms of authority exist in the Church, they are not totally independent of the community. They exist to minister to this community and to some extent they must reflect what the Spirit himself is saying throughout the entire community. It cannot be ignored that devotion to Mary and belief about her role in salvation-history are widespread and ancient, witnessed by the history of the early Church. It is not mature or faithful theology to imply that everything we dislike in the history of Christianity is due to some outside influence while what we approve of is the work of the Holy Spirit. We are here involved in the general problem of authority as a hermeneutic trying to discern what happened in the past in the events of our salvation. We ask how the Spirit allows the scriptural record to be interpreted, and how the Spirit is alive in the world and in the Church today.

(c) Karl Barth pointed out that Mary is intimately involved in the problem of grace. G. Berkouwer discusses at length how the basic problem about Mary is the Catholic understanding of grace. "The central question especially concerns the *elevation of what is creaturely into the super-natural perfection of the life of God* . . . thus Mary as the Mother of God represented our election. Her name is the synopsis of the mystery of faith. . . . It is not difficult to discover that in its Mariology the Roman doctrine of grace is most unshakably manifested."[4] This raises the question: What is grace? What is the Christian life? Is grace something in God or something in the baptized believer? Is grace our passive acceptance by God or is it also our active living out of a Christian life? Is grace response, and is response

4. G. Berkouwer, *The Conflict with Rome* (Grand Rapids: Baker, 1958), p. 174.

active? How does grace work with free will so that it preserves both the autonomy of man (which we see phenomenologically manifested all around us) and preserves the all-important initiative of God (to which the Scriptures bear constant witness)? What does it mean to lead a Christian life? Once we admit that we are justified and sanctified and grant that grace is always given by God, should we not also take seriously the biblical motif of the new creation? Is cooperating with grace (and the imperative to good works under this grace) part of the Christian message? Mary's role in salvation-history depends totally upon her cooperation with grace. The Annunciation can be studied as an absolutely fundamental place where God's initiative and man's free will meet—here at the most important moment of salvation-history. Catholic theology believes, furthermore, that two themes in John—Mary asking for the help of Christ and waiting below the cross—are further illustrations from a particular biblical theology that Mary is actively, although subordinately, involved in the working out of man's salvation.

This is simply a description of the theological problematic on an ecumenical level; it has been improved and crystallized in recent years. The situation, however, has changed significantly with Vatican II. Vatican II took certain theological steps which led to a definite change in attitude towards the Blessed Virgin. From 1962 to 1966 it faced three basic problems in this area. First, the Council was to be a pastoral council and it had to deal with the worship and devotion of Christians throughout the world. Second, it was to be an ecumenical council, and so it had to take seriously the theologies of the churches of the Reformation and the present ecumenical problems and hopes. Third, it was not to be an authoritarian or dogmatic council but rather one which would listen to and serve the new world. The results of Vatican II were that no new dogmas were issued. A dogmatic mentality was not present. The Council was unique inasmuch as it issued an enormous amount of material and yet this material was able to be effective and to cause widespread changes because it was eminently pastoral. It was directed at renewing the Church throughout the world and at the local level. Those theologians who wished more theological elaboration about Mary were, then, quite disappointed. There was no separate constitution on Mary; she was treated within the context of the Church. This itself was of import. It meant that Mary no longer appeared as an independent intermediary or a heavenly or quasi-divine being. She was placed within the context of all Christians. She is the first of Christians, the mother of Christ, and the mother of his Mystical Body, the Church. But she exists basically within the Church and is one of us.

The *Constitution on the Church* when treating of Mary begins with the Annunciation. Through grace and faith Mary received the Word of God spoken to her and consented to give life to the world. But, the Council emphasizes, she was "one with all human beings in their need for salvation."[5] Mary's active role in salvation-history is drawn from the events of the gospel where she acts as mother and as companion of Jesus. The document makes it quite clear that "we have but one Mediator." Yet Mary, in a completely subordinate role and in a way fully comparable to the Incarnation, can pray for men. Her union with her Son must be recognized as efficacious in this secondary way as our salvation-history continues in a dialogue which goes beyond those alive on earth right now. "Mary figured profoundly in the history of salvation and in a certain way unites and mirrors within herself the central truths of the faith. . . . The Virgin Mary in her own life lived an example of that maternal love by which all should be fittingly animated who cooperate in the apostolic mission of the Church on behalf of the rebirth of men." Devotion to Mary is legitimate, but the Council makes it clear that this is never to be in the least way equated with worship of God and Christ. The Council asks every Catholic to "painstakingly guard against any word or deed" which would shock Protestants or non-Christians.

5. The following citations are from Vatican II, "The Role of the Blessed Virgin Mary, Mother of God, in the Mystery of Christ and the Church," *Dogmatic Constitution on the Church,* chapter 8. See Walter M. Abbott, S. J., ed., *The Documents of Vatican II* (New York: America Press, 1966), pp. 85–96.

The *New Catechism,* the English translation of the contro-versial Dutch catechism, is another illustration of the new em-phasis (without total discontinuity) in Catholic attitudes. It keeps Mary as its perspective *within* the community of Chris-tians—past and present.

> The early Church had the mother of Jesus in its midst. As apostolic times go on, the Church speaks more and more about her. The latest gospels, Luke and John, speak of her at the most important places. . . . The Church of which Mary is the image consists of all of us. In this sense Mary is our sister. But the Church is also a mother for each of us. And in this sense Mary is our mother, since she is the living personification of the Church. We can address her with confi-dence, if this helps us to see Jesus with new eyes and reach him more easily. The life of the people of God in the East and in the West has, in fact, shown that this has been a way to the Lord. The believer hears Jesus saying to him: Son, behold your mother. But there are also the words: Mother, behold your son. Mary cherishes the children of the Church. Our salvation is not only sublimer, but also more human, than we think.[6]

I quote this entire passage, in its remarkable theological sim-plicity, to give an example of how traditional elements have been given a freer, more evangelical perspective—yet, without uprooting the Catholic tradition found in the history of the Eastern and Western churches as well as in Martin Luther.

The ecumenical problematic was given further light with Vatican II's *Decree on Ecumenism.* It states that there is a hier-archy of truths within the confession of the Roman Catholic church. Some beliefs are more central and more crucial than others.[7] It remains to be seen how this relatively revolutionary statement will be worked out. It is, moreover, an affirmation which every confession must take seriously, asking not only whether it affirms a theoretical freedom and Christocentricity in its theology but whether this is effectively true in parochial practice.

Finally, the renewal of the liturgy both during and since the Council retains its momentum of creativity, experimentation,

6. *New Catechism* ("Dutch Catechism") (New York: Herder & Herder, 1968), p. 212.
7. Vatican II, *Decree on Ecumenism,* chapter 2, paragraph 11. See Abbott, *The Documents of Vatican II,* p. 354.

and updating. The renewal of the liturgy had, apparently, very definite effects upon devotion to the Blessed Virgin. Surveys have shown that the number of weekly parochial devotions offered throughout the United States have dropped as much as seventy percent during the years following the Council. This neither indicates some growing antagonism towards the mother of Christ, nor a loss of faith; nor is it without theological significance. It indicates that Catholics in general found a certain overemphasis on Mary. More, it is explicable in terms of the reform of the liturgy. As long as the mass was in Latin and without participation, the religious drives which express themselves in singing and in more informal means of worship were channeled away from the central liturgical act to devotions. These were held in English and contained greater liturgical dialogue and contact with the people. When the liturgy was put into the vernacular, made less formal, developed in terms of spontaneity and creativity, there was no reason for "paraliturgical" devotions to supply this need. The new liturgy was celebrated in the evening as well as in the morning, on weekday nights as well as Sunday morning. There could be "guitar masses" for the young, home masses for neighborhoods, underground masses for the daring or the alienated. In short, this ongoing liturgical explosion, while emphasizing more closely the humanity of worship and the immanence of that mysterious Being we call God, also rearranged some of the patterns of Catholic devotional life. It is not yet clear what role Mary, the Apostles and Evangelists, the saints of antiquity and today, will play.

It is significant that Vatican II introduced a new interest in man. Its *Pastoral Constitution on the Church in the Modern World* begins with a lengthy analysis, a theology of man. It then describes how the Church must be in dialogue with man. Theologians such as Karl Rahner and Edward Schillebeeckx now call for a Christian anthropology. Christian theology, without losing respect for the Scriptures and the intervention of God in our world, is nevertheless a man-centered theology. It draws its categories, its words, and its ideas from the world of man as it exists today. Certainly, one of the tasks of the Church is to allow man—in a world of change and technology—to continue to be human by placing the Virgin Mary within the context of Christian men and women. The Church must offer new directions towards this biblical and Christian humanism. Mary appears as a model and resource for those facing the problems of being a woman in the contemporary world. How to be a Christian, how to be a woman—these are the questions with which any contemporary Roman Catholic understanding of Mary, whether it is in the devotional life of the parish or in the theological examination of the events surrounding Jesus Christ, must begin.

The previous remarks are aimed at showing how the ecumenical dialogue in this area is continuing. Dr. Oberman's essay concentrates on Mary in the history of Christian theology. As I have noted, he rightly situates Mary in wider Christian contexts. Apart from the superficial identifications of devotion to Mary with similar ambiguous phenomena from pagan religions, three other questions come to mind.

Dr. Oberman makes a very sharp distinction between *kerygma* and *didache* ("proclamation" and "teaching") and would thereby imply that *didache* is a later and less certain addition. Although this distinction can be a real and valuable one, radical conclusions drawn from it are not supportable. There is no preaching devoid of teaching any more than there is a revelation devoid of human theologizing. Without negating such distinctions, we can understand the New Testament and its milieu only if we approach them while realizing the amount of interplay, continuity, and development present, as well as the differences. Here it is a question of relating all of a gospel to its more essential parts, of relating subsequent (but not always "late" or "apocryphal") teaching to the core of the first preaching. Defining words and trends is necessary; using the words as sole criteria for judgments with extensive ramifications is going too far from the biblical text.

Related to this is a certain a priori skepticism about the truth of some elements of the wider Catholic tradition. This skepticism manifests itself in an uncertainty about when to understand a passage alone, and when to understand it in its context or in the context of other biblical sections. Dr. Oberman (and this is not infrequent among Protestant schools of exegesis) does not really seem to have a constant hermeneutical principle, a methodology for making a consistent evaluation of scriptural texts. We are told that certain passages and certain interpretations are either acceptable or to be rejected; but we are not told why this is so *from the strictly biblical perspective.*

Finally, Dr. Oberman speaks of two approaches to Scripture: the one is analytic (Protestant); the other is synthetic (Catholic). I would admit that Roman Catholic dogmatic theologians to a great extent during the centuries leading up to Vatican II did approach the Scriptures as a source of support for their already "certain" conclusions. Similarly, the approach of liberal Protestant exegesis from D. F. Strauss to Rudolf Bultmann with its valuable crystallization in form criticism is analytic. However, this terminology, too, seems *démodé.* Critical biblical studies and the frequent new joint texts of the Bible show that both Catholic and Protestant exegetes accept a general method vis-à-vis the scriptural text. The approach is critical, historical, and analytic. But exegetes and theologians in the different Christian churches realize also that these elements alone are not enough. It is precisely Bultmann, by carrying the critical-historical method to its extremes and by seeing all of the New Testament as theology, who has raised the questions of faith, Church, and Spirit in our understanding the Scriptures. Scripture is not independent. We are at the mercy of its writers and the early communities they represented. Scripture is neither a purely historical record, nor is it a faith-witness independent of any events. The scientific approach to Scripture is necessary but it is as one-sided as the overly credible fundamentalist view. We are, then, in search of a new hermeneutical method: one which will bring into correct balance, position, and relationship the four elements of text, faith, community, and Spirit. This is no longer a race or a struggle between churches. It is a joint project. It is illustrated by the different and somehow partial approaches of Catholics and Protestants to the role of Mary as witnessed by the New Testament. This joint project can attain some measure of achievement only if the heritage and richness of the different Christian traditions can be brought to bear— in the constellation of text, faith, community, and Spirit—upon the problem of Scripture.

So, we see that the problem of the mother of Jesus concludes as it began—with two basic theological problems stemming from the Reformation: the problem of interpreting Scripture and the understanding of grace and justification. Yet, it is equally clear that in the past ten years enormous progress has been made. This is progress not toward one solution at the expense of the other but toward the best of both.

The author of this essay, Heiko Augustinus Oberman, studied at Sekolah Tinggi in Indonesia, Oxford University, and the University of Utrecht where he received his doctorate in theology *cum laude* in 1957. He came to the Divinity School, Harvard University, in 1958 and became Winn Professor of Ecclesiastical History. In 1966 he left Harvard to become Director of the Institute for Late Medieval and Reformation Studies at Tübingen University. His publications include *The Harvest of Medieval Theology, Forerunners of the Reformation,* and numerous articles on various aspects of the history of Christian thought.

THOMAS F. O'MEARA, O.P.

Aquinas Institute of Theology
Dubuque, Iowa
Spring, 1971

THE VIRGIN MARY IN
EVANGELICAL PERSPECTIVE

Presuppositions

THERE are a number of presuppositions which cannot be argued here in detail—at least not within the narrow confines of a single essay. However, we shall try in what follows to make these presuppositions as explicit as possible.

1. The first and most basic one is the assumption that an evangelical theology properly so called is executed in obedience to Holy Scripture, in communion with the Fathers, and in responsibility to the Brethren.

2. Through the sacrament of Baptism one is placed in this *communio sanctorum,* the *kaine ktisis* or new reality[1] which exists and radiates in three concentric circles: *kerygma, didache* and *leitourgia.* Through Baptism the Christian participates in the three corresponding offices of prophet, doctor and priest.

3. The *kerygma* is constitutive of the Church. It is preserved and handed down through *didache.* It is celebrated or activated —the original sense of its probable root *celer* means "full of

1. "The tangible reality of the Sacraments became the vehicle by which it could be said that the Kingdom had come, and yet was still to come." Krister Stendahl, "Theology and Liturgy," *The Living Liturgy,* ed. ULCA, Department of Worship (Ft. Wayne, 1960), p. 12. Ernst Käsemann does not futurize eschatology and warns us explicitly to interpret the *gewandelte Existenz* as merely a new *sittliche Gesinnung.* "Denn das eschatologische Geschehen besteht gerade darin, dass Gott angefangen hat, die ihm gehörende Welt für sich zurückzugewinnen." Ernst Käsemann, "Gottesdienst im Alltag der Welt (zu Rm 12)," *Judentum, Urchristentum, Kirche (Festschrift* for Joachim Jeremias), ed. Walther Eltester (Berlin, 1960), p. 167.

movement"—in formal worship, in the public service of the *communio* to the old reality, and in the Christian life.

4. *Formgeschichte,* and *Traditionsgeschichte,* indicates that the virgin birth does not belong to the *kerygma* but to the form in which the *kerygma* is preserved and transmitted, i.e., to *didache.* The Creed received at Baptism is anchored in the *leitourgia* of the Church as the community of memory and hope.

5. The formula *lex orandi lex credendi* tends to be misleading insofar as it presents *leitourgia* as an authority for faith instead of as its activation—as a normative rule instead of as the Church's very breath of life.[2] "The formula *lex orandi est lex credendi* means nothing else than that theology is *possible* only within the Church, i.e., as a fruit of this new life in Christ, granted in the sacramental *leitourgia*. . . ."[3]

6. The history of Mariology shows that the proper order of the concentric circles, *kerygma, didache, leitourgia,* has been reversed. Popular Marian devotion was able to influence first *didache* and then *kerygma*—the latter understood as *depositum fidei*—and ultimately to be defined in 1854 and 1950. The way to these developments was paved by the Latin interpretation of *lex orandi lex credendi.*

7. Our last preliminary observation is concerned with the final part of the above description of a truly evangelical theology: to be executed "in responsibility to the Brethren." It has been observed that Mariology is a Roman Catholic problem which has no bearing on the Reformation tradition. Three considerations would seem to expose this attitude as indefensible and—as the conclusion of this essay shall suggest—even dangerous.

2. Yves M.-J. Congar points to this assumption when he says: "Que la liturgie soit un 'lieu théologique' privilegié, le fait est trop bien connu et aujourd'hui trop generalement reconnu pour qui'il soit utile de l'établir." *La Tradition et les Traditions* II, *Essai Théologique* (Paris, 1963), p. 117. We should note here the Orthodox critique on this typically Latin approach to *leitourgia* by Dean Alexander Schmemann: "Liturgical tradition is not an 'authority' or a *locus theologicus*; it is the ontological condition of theology, of the proper understanding of kerygma." "Theology and Tradition," *Worship in Scripture and Tradition,* ed. Massey H. Shepherd (New York, 1963), p. 175.
3. Schmemann, p. 175.

First, while we respect the basic differences between West and East,[4] it cannot be ignored that Mariology in the Orthodox and Roman Catholic traditions, constituting two-thirds of Christendom, is a challenge which has to be answered by every new generation of children of the Reformation.

Granted that this may still be no more than a quantitative argument, never convincing for those who know that at times God upheld his Church as a "remnant,"[5] the relevance of this first consideration may yet appear in the light of a second one.

The "Brethren" to whom the theologian is committed in responsibility cannot possibly be limited to members of one's own denomination; this title should be extended to all baptized Christians and baptizing communities, the Christian churches.[6] Exposed to the various traditions within the World Council of Churches and the forces of renewal within modern Roman Catholicism, we are granted the great privilege, not given in the same degree to the preceding generations, of being transposed into the situation of the first generation of Reformers, who were not primarily founders of new denominations but *doctores* of the Catholic Church[7] calling for reformation exactly on the basis of their responsibility to all catholic Christians.[8]

---

4. Reading, e.g., the *Eastern-Rite Prayers to the Mother of God,* one is struck by the theocentric character of Eastern Mariology, where the Virgin Mary is consistently made transparent, never detaching her from the glory of God. Translated and edited by John H. Ryder (New York, 1955).

5. Cf. Martin Luther: "Si enim solus essem in toto orbe terrarum, qui retinerem verbum, solus essem ecclesia et recte iudicarem de reliquo toto mundo, quod non esset ecclesias." *Weimar Ausgabe* 42. 334. Cf. Calvin in his "Prefatory Address to King Francis": ". . . interdum etiam ecclesiae suae exteriorum notitiam ab hominum aspectu auferat." *Opera Calvini* II (Brunsvigae, 1869), p. 23.

6. This is not meant to deny that in *leitourgia* Christian action is included which bridges church and world and that there is a place for apologetic theology which assumes responsibility for the "Brethren" in a universal sense.

7. Martin Chemnitz finds the very basis for the continuity of God's vocation of true *doctores* in the catholicity of the Church: "Quia enim Ecclesia est Catholica Deus semper excitavit in diversis locis aliquos. . . ." *Loci theologici* (1591), Hypomnemata VI.

8. In a letter dated January 25, 1521, Luther states: "quidquid scripsi et docui secundum meam conscientiam, juramentum et obligationem, ut indignum doctorem sanctae Scripturae, ad laudem et gloriam Dei, ad salutem et felicitatem Ecclesiae catholicae . . . et ad liberationem totius christianae reipublicae . . . proposuisse et fecisse." *WA* 2. 254.

Both in his doctoral and in his prophetic office Martin Luther understood his own responsibility as extending to the whole Church.[9]

This does not mean that one should not criticize or even reject. But as Karl Barth formulated it in a substantial chapter of his *Church Dogmatics* on "Authority in the Church," there will be ample opportunity for that. The first attitude is not one of critique but of honor and love, not only for the Fathers but also for the Brethren.[10]

The third observation is then that the word "challenge" is far too secular, or rather atheological, to express the meaning of the witness of a part of the Church, be it heretical or catholic in the true sense of the word. To quote Karl Barth again, this challenge is to be considered as "authority" insofar as it is the point of departure for my own confession.[11] The reformed tradition has never lost sight of the fact that the hidden communion of the faithful, and therefore the Church of Jesus Christ, may well extend itself to post-Tridentine Catholicism as much as to Orthodoxy and Neo-Protestantism. A confession can only hope to be catholic when it exposes itself to the whole Church, including its heretical aberrations.[12] It is in this light that it seems appropriate to deal with the theme proposed.

---

9. Cf., e.g., also the excellent article, "Luthers Autorität." by Karl G. Steck, in *Ecclesia semper reformanda,* "Sonderheft" to *Evangelische Theologie* (Munich, 1952), pp. 104–20.

10. One should respect the witness of those "die vor mir in der Kirche waren und mit mir in der Kirche sind . . . als das Zeugnis meiner Väter und Brüder ehren und lieben. . . ." *Kirchliche Dogmatik* I. 2 (Zollikon, 1939), p. 658.

11. Continuation of last quotation: ". . . und so, in seiner damit gesetzten Überlegenheit, werde ich es hören. Indem ich das tue, indem ich der Kirche vor mir und neben mir diese Vorordnung zuerkenne, wird sie mir zur Autorität."

12. We believe it possible that there is a "wenn auch verborgene Gemeinschaft der Heiligen und also Kirche Jesu Christi auch im nachtridentinischen Katholizismus und auch in der neuprotestantischen Abirrung. . . . Wir haben also keinen Anlass, uns bei unserer Frage nach den Vätern der Kirche die Ohren nach irgendeiner Richtung zum vornherein zu verstopfen." Barth, p. 686. Cf. *Confessio Belgica,* art. XXVII.

Problems in Biblical Interpretation

It cannot be our task to present an exhaustive exegesis of all passages in Holy Scripture in which the mother of Jesus Christ is referred to. There are, however, some basic issues which one cannot avoid if one wants to take the principle of "obedience to Holy Scripture" seriously.

1. The problem of the relation of Scripture and tradition underlies the hermeneutical task of every exegete. Within the Roman Catholic communion, however, it has not only become determinative for the development of Mariology, but it can also be shown that the history of Mariology has determined the authority of extrabiblical tradition.[13]

(1) Without closing one's eyes to the variety of Mariological schools and currents within contemporary Roman Catholicism one can find an interpretation of Holy Scripture on the basis of later doctrinal developments and dogmatic decisions which gives Roman Catholic hermeneutics its own character. Whether one turns to Carolus Balic, the President of the Mariological Academy in Rome,[14] or to the progressive theologian Hans Küng,[15] one observes that Holy Scripture is not source but resource, not authoritative evidence but elucidating example. Though Küng calls for an "understanding of Protestant difficulties over the new Marian dogmas," the characteristic Roman Catholic conception of the relation of Scripture and dogma finds expression when he goes on to conclude: "There is still much work to be done on deepening and rounding out the theological and especially the scriptural basis of these dogmas."[16]

13. Cf., e.g., Heiko Oberman, *Harvest of Medieval Theology* (Cambridge, 1963), p. 390.
14. Cf. his "Die sekundäre Mittlerschaft der Gottesmutter. Hat Maria die Verdienste Christi für uns de condigno mitverdient?" in *Wissenschaft und Weisheit* 4 (1937). pp. 1–22; and "La Corédemption de Marie. Le problème central de la mariologie contemporaine" in *Pour le centenaire de Lourdes* (Montreal, 1958). pp. 105–9.
15. Cf. his *Rechtfertigung. Die Lehre Karl Barths und eine katholische Besinnung* (Einsiedeln, 1957), p. 287.
16. Hans Küng, *The Council, Reform and Reunion* (New York, 1961), p. 127.

This formulation points to the erosion of the doctoral office and documents (what we have elsewhere described as the transformation of the vital teaching office of the medieval doctor of Scripture, standing together with the bishop as custodian of the deposit of faith) into the apologete of the Teaching Office of the Church.[17]

(2) The basic difference between the tradition of the Reformation and Roman Catholicism on this point can perhaps best be designated as the difference between an analytic and a synthetic hermeneutic. It can be said that between analytic and synthetic interpretation of biblical and ecclesiastical sources runs the demarcation line dividing Protestant and Roman Catholic scholarship. The Reformation acknowledges the *communio sanctorum* as the *con*text and tradition as the *re*source. At the same time the Reformation builds into its hermeneutics—as did Thomas Aquinas and Nicolaus of Lyra to a certain extent earlier—the two chief principles of the "secular" code of historical inquiry designated by the terms *e mente auctoris* (historical purpose) and the nature of *anachronism* (historical time).[18]

(3) Synthetic interpretation, on the other hand, implies an exegesis of texts in Scripture or tradition. This exegesis has its point of departure in the present understanding of the deposit of faith by the Church, usually based on the immutable identity of truth and the promise of abiding assistance of the Holy Spirit.[19] Though it is the task, then, of the Roman Catholic

17. "Quo Vadis, Petre? Tradition from Irenaeus to *Humani Generis*," *Scottish Journal of Theology* 16 (1963), pp. 252 f.

18. "One of the most characteristic preoccupations of the humanists was their interest in history. Their sense of historical time was largely based upon their researches in philology and their discovery that words could have different meanings in different epochs. Hence was born the notion of anachronism. . . ." Myron P. Gilmore, *Humanists ard Jurists* (Cambridge, Mass., 1963), p. 63. For late medieval parallels see Oberman, pp. 378 f.

19. One of the condemned "Errores Modernistarum" reads: "Ecclesiae interpretatio sacrorum Librorum non est quidem spernenda, subiacet tamen accuratiori exegetarum iudicio et correctioni." *Denz.* 3402. (According to the new numeration of Denzinger, *Enchiridion Symbolorum,* ed. Adolfus Schönmetzer, S.J., 32nd ed. [Freiburg, 1963]). *Humani Generis* (1950) describes the task of the theologian in the following words: "Verum quoque est, theologis semper redeundum esse ad divinae revelationis fontes: eorum enim est iudicare qua ratione ea quae a vivo Magisterio docentur, in Sacris Litteris

theologian to find in Scripture and/or tradition a more or less clear expression of the faith as defined by the *magisterium,* it would be contrary to the facts to state that now ipso facto all Roman Catholic exegetes are apologists rather than biblical scholars. There is a group which is as much committed to the "secular" codes of scholarship as its Protestant counterpart. Even though this group is officially unable to draw from its archaeological, philological, and historical research conclusions which do not find their *norma normans* in the *magisterium,* their findings contribute in this fashion to a better understanding of the sources.

The biblical exegesis, however, that in the past promoted and underlay Mariological developments has to be classified as apologetic rather than as biblical theology.[20] Typical examples of its procedures are the use of biblical passages as illustrative material, allegorical interpretation without a literal basis elsewhere in Holy Scripture, and the use of the so-called Anselmian rule, according to which one should ascribe to the Virgin Mary "so much purity that more than that one cannot possibly imagine except for God."[21] Closely related to this instance of

et in divina 'traditione,' sive explicite sive implicite inveniantur." *Denz.* 3886. The intimate connection between Mariology and the relation of Scripture to tradition has been the impetus for the publication of *Schrift und Tradition* as the first volume in the series *Mariologische Studien* (Essen, 1963); see there especially H. M. Koester, "Der Stand der Frage über das Verhältnis von Schrift und Tradition unter Berücksichtigung der Mariologie," pp. 11–36. When one adds to this the collection of articles published by the "Pontifica Academia Mariana Internationalis," *De Scriptura et Traditione,* ed. C. Balic (Rome, 1963), there is no reason to believe that Father G. Tavard is right in claiming that almost all Catholic theologians have rejected the traditional interpretation of the decree by the Council of Trent. Cf. his statements in *Commonweal,* August, 1963. For the contrary view see the conclusion reached by the Roman Catholic historian and widely acknowledged specialist on the history of the Council of Trent, Hubert Jedin. *Geschichte des Konzils von Trient II, Die erste Trienter Sitzungsperiode 1545/47* (Freiburg, 1957), p. 61.

20. Cf., however, René Laurentin, *Structure et Théologie de Luc 1–2* (Paris, 1957).

21. "Decens erat, ut ea puritate, qua maior sub Deo nequit intelligi, virgo illa niteret." Anselm, *De conceptu virginali,* cap. 18, in *PL* 158, 451A. Cf. Scotus. *Ox.* III, d.3, q.1, contra 2. A variation of this rule is applied in the 1950 definition of the Assumption of the Virgin Mary: "cum eam posset [Redemptor] tam magno honore exornare. ut eam a sepulcri corruptione servaret incolumen, id reapse fecisse credendum est." *Denz.* 3900.

reliance on natural theology is the application of logic as the connection between biblical passages and interpretation. E.g.: The Church is the living Christ (Eph. 1:22), the Virgin Mary is the mother of Christ (Luke 1:36). Ergo: the Virgin Mary is the mother of the Church. It should perhaps be noted that this way of dealing with Holy Scripture as if it were a collection of propositions transcends confessional boundaries.

2. Next to the problem of Roman Catholic hermeneutics as the basis for biblical interpretation we have to concern ourselves with the results of *Traditionsgeschichte* and *Formgeschichte.* We can no longer be satisfied with merely collecting all the biblical statements about the Virgin Mary. A few observations are in order, drawn from recent investigations:

(1) Although the virgin birth is the basis of all the later doctrinal developments, it can no longer be overlooked that only at two places is the virgin birth attested, i.e., in the infancy narrative of Matthew 1–2 and Luke 1. Moreover, these should not be looked upon as two forms of the same story in view of the characteristic differences between them.[22]

(2) It has been suggested that the heading "virgin birth" would be a misleading one for Matthew's presentation. Krister Stendahl comes to the conclusion that we face here "an account which knows of a 'virgin birth,' but the supernatural element is neither stressed nor glorified. It rather has the form of a divine overcoming of a stumbling block and counteracting of misunderstanding and slander."[23] As regards the Lucan account it should be noted that the point of the story is the conception through "overshadowing" by the Holy Spirit: the birth, virginal or not, is not at all mentioned.[24]

---

22. Krister Stendahl, "Quis et Unde? An Analysis of Mt. 1–3," in Eltester, p. 96.
23. *Matthew,* New and Revised edition of Peake's Commentary (Edinburgh, 1962), col. 674i., p. 771.
24. "Das Wunder liegt in der Erzeugung; nicht in der Geburt, die überhaupt nicht erwähnt wird." Martin Dibelius, "Jungfrauensohn und Krippenkind. Untersuchungen zur Geburtsgeschichte Jesu im Lukas Evangelium," *Botschaft und Geschichte, Gesammelte Aufsätze von Martin Dibelius* I, ed. Günther Bornkamm (Tübingen, 1953), p. 16. Cf. p. 78: ". . . hier (Luk 1) steht im Vordergrunde die Botschaft von dem Messias auf Davids Thron, den Gott selber auf wunderbare Weise aus heiligem Geist erschaffen wird."

(3) While the Gospel of Mark does not mention the virgin birth, we find in the Prologue of John the "concept of virgin birth" applied to all the children of God who, notwithstanding their birth from natural parents, have been given "the right to become children of God, not born of any human stock, or by the fleshly desire of a human father but the offspring of God himself."[25] Though Hans von Campenhausen grants that the issue cannot be decided with absolute certainty, he points out that this passage might well be a polemical allusion to an early virgin birth tradition.[26] We choose to omit here a discussion of the six other "children" of Mary (Mark 6:3) among whom Jesus was the "firstborn" (Luke 2:7).

(4) The Pauline corpus does not show any interest in the virgin birth either. The one much discussed text, Gal. 4:4: "God sent his own Son, born of a Woman, born under the law," does not so much contradict the virgin birth tradition because of the use of the word "woman." But the very point Paul wants to make—the depth of the *kenosis* of Christ in order to identify himself with all men under the law—would be lost if he intended to say "born of a virgin."[27]

(5) In the Gospels two attitudes toward the figure of Mary can be discerned. First of all there is the emphasis on the distance between Christ and his mother, not bridgeable by ties of blood but only by ties of faith.

While Jesus is described as a cause of irritation to his environment which knows so well that he is the son of Joseph rather than the expected Messiah (Mark 6:3; cf. John 6:42), Mary herself comes to share this irritation (Mark 3:21; 6:4). The identification of the birth of Christ and the birth of all the faithful as children of God—which we noted in our reference to John 1:12 f.—finds clear expression in Jesus' answer to the

25. *The New English Bible* (Oxford, 1961), John 1:12, 13.
26. ". . . denn einer jungfräuliche Geburt im wörtlichen Sinne, wie sie von andern für Jesus behauptet worden war, wird durch die Ausdehnung der Vorstellung auf die Christen insgesamt vielmehr um ihren Sinn gebracht und zurückgewiesen." *Die Jungfrauengeburt in der Theologie der alten Kirche.* Sitzungsberichte der Heidelberger Akademie der Wissenschaften, Phil. hist. Klasse, Abh. 3 (1962), p. 12.
27. Dibelius, p. 29, n. 47; von Campenhausen, p. 13.

woman who said, "Blessed the womb that carried you and the breasts that suckled you": "No, blessed are those who hear the word of God and keep it" (Luke 11:27 f.). And again, according to Mark 3:32: "Your mother and your brothers are outside asking for you"; to which Jesus answers: "Whoever does the will of God is my brother, my sister, my mother."

The blood relationship is not the basis of but—initially—rather an obstacle to a faith relationship of Mary to Jesus. The tendency to assign the Virgin Mary a supernatural place transcending the level of the faithful, argued on physical-metaphysical grounds, must have been an ancient and a natural inclination. The remarkable unanimity of the Gospels—including John's account of the wedding at Cana (John 2:3–5)—points to the fact that Jesus has consistently answered that faith alone provides a proximity to him in time and space, a relation formulated by Paul as "being in Christ" (Gal. 3:28).

(6) It has been said that the *Magnificat* displays exactly the opposite attitude to the figure of Mary: the Lucan birth narrative puts first on the lips of the angel and then on those of Mary herself a benediction of the mother of Jesus which Jesus so clearly rejected.[28]

Though the *Magnificat* has indeed its own texture and intention, it does not, however, seem to stand opposite to what we described above as a biblical image of Mary nor to continue the "womb theology" rejected by Jesus. The Lucan emphasis falls on the humility of Mary, not on her person but on her office as representative of the remnant of Israel. It is the New Testament reformulation of the Song of Hannah: "the feeble gird on strength . . . the hungry have ceased to hunger . . . the barren has borne seven . . . the Lord brings low, he also exalts . . ." (1 Sam. 2:4–7). The tension between the promise of the angel that Mary shall conceive in her womb and bear a son (Luke 1:31;

28. "Die späten mythischen Stücke über Jesu Herkunft, welche vorliegen, besonders in den lukanischen Vorgeschichten, lassen den Engel und dann im Loblied indirekt sogar Maria selber (Luk 1:48) gerade jene Seligpreisung der Mutter Jesu aussprechen, welche Jesus ganz deutlich abgelehnt hatte." Jakob Amstutz, "Die Verehrung Mariae vom freien Protestantismus gesehen," *Evangelische Marienverehrung, Eine Heilige Kirche* I, ed. Friedrich Heiler and Fr. Siegmund-Schultze (1955–1956), p. 39.

cf. 2:21) with her virginity is one of these signs of God's eschatological initiative,[29] a variation on the theme of Sarah who bears a child in her old age: "And God said to Abraham, 'As for Sarah your wife . . . I will bless her, and she shall be a mother of nations; kings of peoples shall come to her' " (Gen. 17:15, 16). These are the covenantal words to Abraham (Luke 1:55 and 73) which are echoed in the "Blessed are you among women!" (Luke 1:28, 42).

For an understanding of later developments it is important to observe that Luke and Matthew in their birth narratives look in different directions—the first more "dogmatically" interested in how a human being can be the Son of God, the latter more "apologetically" inclined in pointing out that Jesus was the expected Messiah.[30] At the same time Luke is so interested in showing the continuation and fulfillment of the history of salvation in the line Sarah-Hannah-Elizabeth-Mary that one cannot understand this distinction as mutually exclusive. On the contrary it should be seen as a more dogmatic presentation of the same apologetic motive vis-à-vis the unbelieving Jews, a motive which so clearly underlies Matthew's account.[31] This difference between "apologetic" and "dogmatic" is perhaps best clarified by the observation that "in Matthew Joseph is the main person. It is he who receives the revelations and through him the action progresses. . . . In Luke Mary is the recipient of revelation and Joseph is described as he who stands by."[32] One is inclined to observe that whereas within the Protestant tradition

29. Frère Max Thurian has described this very concisely and beautifully in his *Marie Mère du Seigneur-Figure de l'Église* (Taizé, 1962), p. 27. There is, however, a shift of emphasis when he proceeds to meditate on the significance of the virginity of Mary as such: "La Vierge Marie introduit donc en le monde, où le mariage est devenu loi universelle, selon l'ordre de la création, la nouveauté du Royaume de Dieu qui fait irreption avec le Christ. Ainsi la virginité de Marie est un triple signe. . . ," p. 51.

30. "Lukas und Matthäus blicken also in verschiedene Richtungen. . . . Wir können sie kurz als die dogmatische und die 'apologetische' Tendenz bezeichnen," von Campenhausen, p. 20.

31. Only if one underlines the word *ausschliesslich* can one agree with von Campenhausen: "Die Darstellung bei Matthäus ist von vornherein anders gestaltet . . . es geht Matthäus ausschliesslich um den Weissagungsbeweis . . . ," p. 19.

32. Stendahl, "Quis et Unde?" p. 95.

there is a tendency to apply the Matthean Joseph image to the Virgin Mary, within Roman Catholicism there is and has been the inclination to extend the Lucan Mary image to Joseph.[33]

3. Next to the issues of Roman Catholic hermeneutics and *Formgeschichte* there is in the third place the question of Protestant hermeneutics. Concerned to avoid the Docetism of the Spirit which the Reformers found to the right in Counter-Reformation theology and to the left in sections of the Radical Reformation, the Protestant tradition has emphasized that the Spirit speaks *in* the word and that understanding originates from exposure to Scripture rather than from direct illumination, be it individually or collectively received.

Obedience to Holy Scripture as the testimony to and receptacle of what God "in these last days" has spoken by his Son (Heb. 1:2) implies the use of all means to come to an exegesis which is *sachgemäss* or appropriate to its subject matter. The use, e.g., of *Form* and *Traditionsgeschichte* is a basic part of this sober listening to Scripture itself.

At the same time Scripture is understood only in the Church. The Church approaches Scripture not without preconceived ideas, as a *tabula rasa,* but feeds on a whole history of understanding. One may well call this history "Tradition" if one first makes clear that this Tradition is not the *authoritative vehicle of divine truth,* but the *instrumental vehicle of Scripture* which comes alive in a constant dialogue with the faithful.

Protestant hermeneutics has led to certain emphases as regards the interpretation of the place and function of the Virgin Mary, which can be indicated in a few words: the *Magnificat* as a poetic confession of justification *sola gratia* and *sola fide.*[34]

33. This is not a recent development but accompanied and followed both the first declaration of the dogma of the Immaculate Conception promulgated by the Council of Basel, 1439 and the second declaration by Pope Pius IX in 1854. Cf. Geiler of Keisersberg: "Joseph is geheiliget worden in mutterlieb wie Maria," *Evangelibuch,* fol. 157ʳ 1-2; cf. Gerson, *Opera omnia* III, cols. 848 ff. Quoted and discussed by E. Jane Dempsey, *The Doctrine of Justification in the Preaching of Doctor John Geiler of Keisersberg* (Harvard Ph.D.,thesis, 1962), pp. 317 f.

34. Cf. Luther, *WA* 15. 476; 17. II. 399; *WA* 52. 692; Calvin, *Institutes* II. 3. 13; Zwingli, *Corpus Reformatorum, Zwinglii Opera* I. 396 ff. See

She believes the word of the angel and trusts God's promises: she knows that it is God's mercy which made him turn to her. The humility of Mary, then, is not seen as a disposition which provided the basis and reason for God's choice, but is regarded rather as the result of God's election and prevenient grace.

It is clear that not only the view of the relation of Scripture and tradition but also the understanding of justification determines the presentation of the role of the Virgin Mary in the history of salvation. It is on these grounds that, on the one hand, the Roman Catholic Eduard Stakemeier can claim that the catholic elements in the Mariology of the Reformers had to disintegrate,[35] while, on the other hand, the Protestant Roger Mehl can state that Mariology is the focus and locus where all the heresies of Roman Catholicism are welded together.[36] Though in both traditions the Virgin Mary can be regarded as *typus ecclesiae,* the function of *ecclesia* is conceived of in fundamentally different ways.

To summarize the Protestant position on this point, one might well conclude this section by recalling the words of Karl Barth at the end of his discussion of Roman Catholic Mariology: "Revelation and reconciliation are irreversibly, indivisibly and exclusively the work of God."[37]

Eduard Stakemeier. "De Beata Maria Virgine eiusque cultu iuxta Reformatores," *De Mariologia et Oecumenismo,* ed. C. Balic (Rome, 1962), pp. 424–477; *Das Marienlob der Reformatoren.* ed. Walter Tappolet (Tübingen, 1962), esp. the useful index on pp. 357 ff.; Walter Delius, *Geschichte der Marienverehrung* (Basel, 1963), pp. 195–234; Gottfried W. Locher, "Inhalt und Absicht von Zwinglis Marienlehre," *Kirchenblatt für die reformierte Schweiz* 107 (1951), pp. 34–37.

35. "Profunda reformatorum diversitas a mariologia catholica provenit ex principiis reformatoriis et specialiter ex sex dictis 'sola particulis,' " p. 474. On Luther: "Inductus principiis 'solius Scripturae' necnon 'solius Dei operantis,' paulatim tam meritum quam intercessionem Matris Dei negavit eiusque invocationem dissuasit vel exclusit," p. 450. Calvin interprets Scripture and the Fathers "secundum suas praeiudicatas opiniones," p. 460.

36. "C'est pourquoi nous ne pouvons opposer à la mariologie prise dans son ensemble qu'un non résolu. Nous sommes persuadés qu'elle constitue une sorte d'engrenage mortel pour la foi évangelique. En elle se rejoignent toutes les héresies du catholicisme. . . ." *Du Catholicisme Romain. Approche et Interpretation* (Neuchâtel-Paris, 1957), p. 91.

37. Barth, I. 2, p. 160.

Problems in the History of Mariology

It is not our intention to sketch the whole history of Mariology. Instead a selection is made of aspects of this history that seem to have a bearing on a contemporary evangelical approach to Mariology. Accordingly we should like to make some comments on Mariological developments in the early Church, in the Middle Ages, and in the Reformation period in the light of recent investigations.

1. *Early Church.*

(1) In an important article Bishop Paulus Rusch of Innsbruck argues that there are two historical roots of Mariology.[38] The first is a pretheological affection for the Virgin Mary as a mother figure displayed, for example, by the Philomarianites.[39] This group overemphasized the orthodox epithet *Theotokos* to the point that the Virgin came to be looked upon as a deity. Epiphanius of Salamis (†403), reporting on this sect with horror, concludes his description by saying: "They should not say: 'We honor the queen of heaven.' "[40] Asceticism is designated by Bishop Rusch as the second root, the cradle of true Marian devotion, where the praise of the Virgin is directed towards her as the prototype of virginity. This emphasis was retained by the monastic movement. Bishop Rusch goes on to observe that in the fifth century heretics are the first to defend Mariological theses, which later came to be generally accepted; for example, the representatives of Docetism defend the virginity of Mary *post partum,* while the Pelagians maintain the doctrine of her complete sinlessness. Moreover, the first to uphold the Immaculate Conception was again a Pelagian, Julian of Eclanum (†454).[41]

38. "Mariologische Wertungen," *Zeitschrift für katholische Theologie* 85 (1963), pp. 129–61.
39. More often called "Kollyridians." See *Lexikon für Theologie und Kirche* VI (1961), pp. 328 f.; Delius, p. 100.
40. *Haereses,* 79.8, ed. K. Holl, in *Die griechischen christlichen Schriftsteller der ersten drei Jahrhunderte* 37. 483; quoted by Delius, p. 331.
41. Rusch, p. 138; cf. p. 158: "Ja, es trat das Überraschende zu Tage dass Irrlehrer im Altertum nicht selten eine später anerkannte mariologische These, etwa die Pelagianer die unbefleckte Empfängnis, vorwegnahmen." Rusch refers to R. Laurentin, *La Vierge Marie: Initiation théologique* IV (Paris,

For our purposes it is important to observe that in the light of the foregoing, the rejection by Nestorius († c. 451) of the title *Theotokos* for the Virgin Mary appears in a new light. Traditionally Nestorius is presented as a heretic who with christological motivations accidentally seized on the title of the Virgin Mary with the purpose of declaring that there are two separate Persons in the Incarnate Christ.[42] It may well be closer to the truth, however, to say that Nestorius, setting out on a purposeful crusade against a heretical Mariology, accidentally compromised himself as regards Christology. Bishop Rusch, indeed, suggests that Nestorius turned against a tendency to interpret the *Theotokos* title so that Mary would be the mother of God not only according to the humanity of Christ (*secundum humanitatem*), as Chalcedon had stated, but also according to the divinity of Christ (*secundum divinitatem*), in the same way as there are mothers of gods in pagan religions.[43] The *Theotokos* title, therefore, as upheld by the Council of Ephesus (431) and interpreted by the Council of Chalcedon (451), should not be isolated from its historical context, but regarded as the *via media* between a paganizing Mariological heresy and a Nestorianizing christological heresy. Where the first aspect is ignored, as is usually the case, the ambivalence of the title *Theotokos* is overlooked, and the term itself then necessarily leads to new Mariological heresies.

(2) A second recent study dealing with the pre-Chalcedonian period alerts us to the fact that the virginity of Mary, as in the creedal clause *natus ex Maria Virgine,* is genetically seen not to be regarded as the safeguard of an orthodox approach to the mystery of the Incarnation. This is a matter of later interpretation.

1956), pp. 261 ff. P. Pourat points out that in the East Marian devotion was at times an indication of heresy: *La spiritualité chrétienne* I, (Paris, 1947), p. 477; quoted by Rusch, p. 130, n. 6.
42. Berthold Altaner, *Patrologie* (Freiburg, 1958), p. 302; J. N. D. Kelly, *Early Christian Doctrines* (New York, 1958), pp. 301 ff.
43. "Es gab eine Bestrebung, Maria zur Gottesmutter im heidnischen Sinn zu erklären, also *secundum deitatem,* wie es denn in den heidnischen Religionen eigentliche Mütter von Göttern gab. Dagegen hatte sich Nestorius gewandt und war debei in das Gegenteil geraten . . . ," p. 139; Laurentin, p. 262.

The belief in the virginity of the mother of Jesus, of which we traced the beginnings in the birth narratives of Matthew and Luke, could not possibly have determined the course the second-century Church should take, surrounded as it was by Jews, Jewish Christians and Adoptionists on the one side and various schools of Gnostics on the other side. Over against the Gnostics the catholic theologians were concerned to "defend," as Hans von Campenhausen points out, the reality of a "truly and in the full sense of the word human birth, not really a virginal birth." And over against the Judaizing wing the catholic apologetes are "above all interested in emphasizing the pre-temporal birth of the Son, i.e., in his preexistence, and again therefore not in the birth from a virgin."[44]

The virgin birth could not be the necessary means, therefore, for preserving the true meaning or the full reality of the self-identification of God with the world,[45] for which it has later so often been held by Roman Catholic and Protestant orthodoxy. It has rather to be seen, as we noted above, as a sign of God's eschatological action, to be grasped in faith, at once more hidden *and* the culmination point of the same line running from Sarah and Hannah to Elizabeth and Mary. The absence of an inherent, systematic necessity of the virgin birth is well expressed by Martin Luther, who, while personally holding not only the virgin birth but also the perpetual virginity of Mary, could say: "It is not that important whether she is a virgin or a woman. . . ."[46]

44. Von Campenhausen, *Jungfrauengeburt,* p. 18.

45. "Die Jungfrauengeburt is eben nicht einer theologischen Tendenz zuliebe formuliert worden. Sie ist einfach ein überkommenes vermeintlich 'apostolisches' Stück biblischer Überlieferung," ibid.

46. "Nihil dictum de matre, quia. sicut supra dixi, leyt nit vil dran, an sit virgo vel femina, quamquam deus voluit virginem esse," *WA* 15. 411. Gerhard Ebeling regards this statement as "die extremste Aussage" of Luther on this point and as an "okkamistische Rekurs auf die potentia dei ordinata." *Evangelische Evangelienauslegung: Eine Untersuchung zu Luthers Hermeneutik* (Darmstadt, 1962), p. 247. However, Luther writes this as a comment on Matthew 2:6, which deals with the fulfillment of the Old Testament and of Israel. In *this* context the distinction between woman and virgin is not crucial. The last five words of the above Luther quotation should be "lightly read," as an appended afterthought.

(3) We have noted the theological ambivalence of the *Theotokos* title and the pretheological token character of the virginity of Mary. It is important to note in a last comment on the beginnings of Mariology in the early Church that with the progress of time the "dogmatic" element in the Lucan account becomes more prominent at the expense of the "apologetic" tendency which we found to underlie both Matthew 1 and Luke 1. Ignatius of Antioch († c. 115), the only "Apostolic Father" to teach the virgin birth,[47] can be looked upon as a representative of the "dogmatic" school of thought. Justin Martyr († c. 165), on the other hand, can be regarded as perhaps the last representative of the purely "apologetic" approach.[48] At the end of the second century these two currents meet in Irenaeus († c. 200). His contrast between the obedient Mary and the disobedient Eve,[49] placed within the context of his recapitulation theory, can serve to show both the fulfillment of the Old Testament and the inner connection between Adam's formation out of virginal earth with Christ's birth from a Virginal Woman. There is no sign yet of the later identification of the Virgin Mary with the Church or with the heavenly Jerusalem which seems to stem from Manichean sources.

At the end of the second century a new element is introduced into the discussion. Whereas we saw that Matthew dealt with the question *Quis* and *Unde,* "Who is Christ" and "Whence did he come,"[50] and that Luke added the question *Qua,* "In what manner"[51] could Mary be the mother of Christ, increasingly the interest now turns to the question *Quo,* "By what means" and "To what purpose."[52] The attention begins to

47. Robert M. Grant has a more than usually high regard for the witness of Ignatius since he "preserved apostolic tradition as it had been interpreted at Antioch in the generation before him." "Hermeneutics and Tradition in Ignatius of Antioch. A methodological investigation," *Archivo di Filosofia* 1–2 (1963), p. 200.

48. For this and the following see von Campenhausen, pp. 22 ff., and Delius, pp. 34–103.

49. ". . . Maria virgo oboediens . . . Eva vero inobaudiens . . . ," *Contra Haereses* III. 22. 4.

50. Cf. Stendahl, "Quis et Unde?"

51. As in the school example: "illuc qua veniam?"

52. As in: "quo mihi prodest?"

focus on the person of Mary herself, her eminent purity and sanctity as prerequisite for the Incarnation and ascetic example for the Christian community. In view of the programmatic asceticism of Gnosticism this new development could not take place till after the threat of Gnosticism had subsided.[53] We do not here follow this development from the *Protoevangelium Iacobi* (before 200 A.D.) into Alexandrian theology in the East and the pre-Augustinian theology of Ambrose and Jerome. The spread of the monastic movement and the anthropological pre-suppositions leading to the identification of sexuality with sin made for a moralizing elevation of the Virgin Mary which finds its clearest expression in the *semper virgo* doctrine, Mary's virginity *ante-, post-partum* and even *in partu.*

While the questions *Quis, Unde* and *Qua* had been concerned with Jesus Christ, the question *Quo* is aimed towards his mother and thus forms the basis for what we have come to know as Mariology. While the references by Matthew and Luke to the virgin birth had been christological devices, a part of the *didache* meant to preserve and transmit the *kerygma,* there are clear indications that by the end of the second century Mariology started to become part of the *kerygma* itself: the sign becomes the thing signified. Time and again we get a glimpse of the impact of *leitourgia* on this development. A virtue-centered interpretation of the *Magnificat,* perhaps part of "the" early Christian hymnbook, and the spread of private Marian devotions led in the fifth century to the incorporation of Marian feasts into the liturgical calendar, which in turn could later serve as a point of departure for further Mariological developments.

2. *Middle Ages and Reformation.*

(1) It is not strange that Mariology was able to develop so strikingly in the Middle Ages—in other respects not dogmatically productive—because of Christ's receding into heaven, sitting at the right hand of the Father, preparing for his return

53. On sexual asceticism in the early Church see Hans von Campenhausen, "Die Askese im Urchristentum." *Tradition und Leben. Kräfte der Kirchengeschichte* (Tübingen, 1960), pp. 133–53. In Corinth St. Paul was confronted with "Gnostische Ideale eines asketischen Übermenschentums," ibid., p. 139.

to judge the quick and the dead. In the confrontation with Arianism in the East the divinity of Christ had to be strongly emphasized, and thus the figure of the cosmic Christ, the *Pantocrator,* had become prominent. In the West the Crucifixion rather than the Incarnation became the living center of Christology. But even so, according to the influential Anselmian interpretation, the Atonement took place in the realm between Christ and God. The Atonement is more the basis for the efficaciousness of the sacraments than the event through which men in Christ have "free access" to God. In other words, Christ's mediation is largely restricted to the cross.

Due to theological difficulties so eloquently formulated by Bernard of Clairvaux and Thomas Aquinas, the Immaculate Conception was not promulgated till 1439 (by the Council of Basel in a session which remained unconfirmed) and the relation of Mary's death to her corporeal assumption was not yet sufficiently or convincingly clarified.[54] But both doctrines were strongly supported on the eve of the Reformation.[55] Two themes in particular seem to contribute to the centrality of the place and function of the Virgin Mary. There is first the theme of Mary's assumption, her reception into heaven, and reunion with her Son. In his welcoming speech Christ announces that he will share the Kingdom of his Father with her; Mary will rule the kingdom of Mercy and thus become *Mater misericordiae;* Christ will reign in the kingdom of Truth and Justice and therefore function as the *iudex vivorum et mortuorum.*[56] A fifteenth-century miniature presents, under the title "Mary mediator between God and man," the Queen of Heaven as protecting the faithful under her skirts from a God who tries to find a target for the arrow, ready on his bow, among those faithful who dare to venture out from under Mary's protection.[57] Most

54. Cf. Carolus Balic, *Testimonia de Assumptione B.V.M. ex omnibus saeculis* I (Rome, 1948).
55. For the following, cf. the chapter on "Mariology" in Oberman, pp. 281–321.
56. Cf. Oberman, p. 311.
57. *Speculum humanae salvationis* (Munich, 1585). The following statement by Jaroslav Pelikan. therefore, requires clarification: "The cult of the Blessed Virgin Mary has likewise helped to soften the harsh picture of God which

prominent are the breasts of the Virgin, which suggest that the angry God figure is the Son, since according to popular tradition Mary shows her breasts to her Son, who in turn intercedes with the Father.

(2) The second theme is of a more strictly theological nature. The argument is that the Virgin Mary is *pura creatura* or *homo purus,* here not in the sense that she is pure as regards original sin but pure in the sense of "real": she is a real creature or truly man. This now is contrasted with Christ who is not *homo purus* but *homo deus*: Christ is not pure nature because his humanity is united in hypostatic union with the Godhead. In contrast to Mary, Christ did not, therefore, really and fully belong to mankind. The term "pure nature" serves here as a basis for establishing a gulf between Christ and mankind which can be bridged only by the Virgin Mary: the foundation for man's *fiducia,* his confident hope for eternal life, is therefore the resurrection of the Virgin Mary rather than the resurrection of Christ.

Because of her "breasts" related to God, and because of her "pure nature" related to man, the Virgin Mary can occupy that place of mediation which in classical orthodox theology had been held by Jesus Christ.

(3) For the Reformers, Mariology could not possibly be a side issue since it touched so directly on their common main theme, the redemption by God in Jesus Christ. All three major Reformers, Martin Luther, Huldrich Zwingli, and John Calvin, retained important elements of the early Church tradition but rejected unanimously the medieval developments as sketched above in the two themes of "mother of mercy" and "pure nature."

Luther's translation of the hymn by Venantius Fortunatus, *Agnoscat omne saeculum,* "Der aller Weltkreis nie beschloss der liegt nun in Mariae Schoss,"[58] could perhaps best serve as

prophetic religion so frequently produces." *The Riddle of Roman Catholicism* (New York, 1959), p. 139.

58. ". . . quem totus orbit non capit, portant puellae viscera"; He whom the whole world could not contain [and: grasp!] is now in Mary's womb. *WA* 35. 435.

the heading for his interpretation of the role of the Virgin Mary. The Virgin Mary is the sign of the exinanition of God. For Luther she is the Virginal Mother, the *Theotokos,* and even the perpetual Virgin,[59] but all these titles are conferred upon her against the background of a reinterpretation of the *Magnificat.*[60] There is indeed little chance that Mary can become the thing signified rather than the sign when one can let her say as Luther did: "I am only the workshop in which God operates."[61]

The warm praise which Luther has for the mother of God throughout his life, his last sermon on January 17, 1546 included,[62] is not based upon the great qualities of Mary herself but on the grace granted to her. As a person, Luther can say, the Virgin Mary is not greater than Mary Magdalene, the sinner, since through faith all Christians are equal.[63]

When Luther in 1535 attacks the theme of Mary, the mother of mercy, as contrasted with Christ, the judge,[64] this is not an ad hoc reference but the outgrowth and application of his discovery of the meaning of *iustitia.* In his *Commentary on the Psalms,* 1513–15, Luther insists that in Christ mercy and righteousness are united.[65] When one destroys this unity, Christ is no longer *veritas* but has become se*veritas*!

Luther also rejects the implications of the second medieval theme noted above. The very point of his doctrine of the Incarnation is that God emptied himself to become man, truly man. The contrast between Mary as *purus homo* and Christ as

59. *WA* 11. 320.

60. Cf. H. D. Preuss, *Maria bei Luther* (Gütersloh, 1954), and Tappolet, esp. pp. 58 ff.

61. "Ego nihil sum quam fabrica, in qua Deus operatur. . . ." *WA* 7. 573.

62. *WA* 51. 128.

63. 1525: *WA* 10. I. 2. 432.

64. *WA* 41. 199.

65. " 'Iustitia et pax osculatae sunt' quia idem Christus est utrumque." Ps. 84 (85): 11; *WA* 4. 16. Cf. Heinrich Bornkamm, "Zur Frage der Iustitia Dei beim Jungen Luther," *Archiv für Reformationsgeschichte,* 52 (1961), p. 28. This reference functions in Bornkamm's presentation as one of his effective arguments against Ernst Bitzer's thesis. according to which Luther's "breakthrough" should not be dated before 1518. *Fides ex auditu* (Neukirchen, 1958), esp. p. 101.

homo deus could not be more alien to his thought. It is impossible that *fiducia* should be placed in Mary—and, of course, even more impossible that a greater *fiducia* should be invested in Mary than in Christ—since *fiducia* can be used synonymously with what traditionally is known as *latreia*: "For *fiducia* is the highest honor, due only to God, who alone is truth."[66]

(4) As is usually the danger in describing the position of the Reformation, one is tempted to highlight and therefore to overemphasize those points on which the preceding tradition is rejected. Rather than showing how far Zwingli and Calvin shared Luther's critique, we prefer to call attention in a final comment to the positive elements in the attitude of these Reformers to the Virgin Mary.

Zwingli defends in 1529 the use of the Ave Maria, not as a prayer but as praise "in order to salute and laud Mary."[67] He feels that the best way to honor the mother of God is to imitate her virtues.[68] Instead of the usual medieval tendency he *asso-*

66. 1522: "Nam fiducia est summus honor Deo soli debitus, qui solus est veritas." *WA* 10. II. 166. One should compare a hymn in the *Crailsheimer Schulordnung* of 1480 with Luther's interpretation:

"Sancta Maria steh uns bey
so wir sullen sterben.
Mach uns aller sunden frey
und lass uns nicht verderben.
Vor dem teufel uns bewar
rayne magt Maria,
hilff uns an der engelschar
so singen wir alleluia."

Friederich Spitta, *Ein fester Burcht ist unser Gott* (Göttingen, 1905), p. 268. See Luther's interpretation in his *Trinitatislieder*:

"Gott der Vater wohn uns bei
und lass uns nicht verderben
mach uns aller sünden frei
und helf uns selig sterben.
Für dem Teufel uns bewahr
halt uns bei festem Glauben
und auf dich lass uns bauen
aus Herzensgrund vertrauen . . .
"Jesus Christus wohn uns bei . . . etc."
"Heilig Geist wohn uns bei . . . etc."

WA 35. 450. Cf. Spitta, p. 266.

67. *CR, Zwinglii Opera,* I. 408.

68. Cf. Stakemeier, p. 457. His discussion of Zwingli needs correction on several points. Most important is that his observation that "Zwinglius sibi

ciates Mary and Christ to the point where he can say: "The more honor and love for Christ, the more also the esteem and honor for Mary, since she has borne us such a great and at the same time merciful Lord and Redeemer."[69]

While Calvin points to the danger of honoring the Virgin Mary as person rather than as elected instrument, he insists on the close connection between Mary and Christ: "Today we cannot celebrate the blessing given us in Christ without commemorating at the same time how high an honor God has granted to Mary when he chose to make her the mother of his only Son."[70] In a comment on Luke 1:43[71] Calvin gives us the opportunity to see his standards for a proper esteem for the Virgin Mary more clearly than anywhere else. He finds in Elizabeth's praise for Mary the true *via media* between shying away from "honor where honor is due" and superstitious adoration. "There are few who do not fall into one of these two sins, since at the one side there are those who are so extremely pleased with themselves that they cannot stand the gifts of God to their Brethren; at the other side there are those who adore human beings so superstitiously that they make deities out of them." And again: "Elizabeth takes the *via media* which we should follow: i.e., she honors the Virgin, inasmuch as Mary was honored by God. . . . But at the same time she does not stop at this point . . . she shows that the Virgin Mary has no dignity of herself but that rather everything hinges on God's wish to accept her."[72]

Indeed, the Reformers wanted to safeguard the true measure of honor due to Mary because of the close connection with a

conscius est Scripturam solam non sufficere ad stricte probandam perpetuam Beatae Mariae virginitatem" is argued on the basis of an incomplete citation which omits the contrary proof, p. 453. See *Huldreich Zwinglis Werke,* ed. Melchior Schuler and Johannes Schulthes (Zurich, 1828 ff.), V. 617 and VI. 205–6. See further, Locher, p. 36: "Zwingli hat den Einwand gekannt. . . . Er ist ihm mit Entschiedenheit entgegengetreten. . . ."

69. *CR, Zwinglii Opera,* I. 427 f.

70. *Harmonia Evangelica,* comment on Luke 1:42; *CR* 45. 35.

71. Ibid.

72. *CR* 46. 107.

true understanding of the person and work of Jesus Christ.[73] True worship is true knowledge and vice versa.

In their pastoral concern for all the Brethren the Reformers made themselves responsible for the true understanding of the Christian faith even on the most popular level, no longer willing to allow for the gulf between a thinking man's faith and "vulgar" Catholicism. When this is threatened, Luther can exclaim as he did in 1523: "I could wish that the cult of Mary would be completely abrogated, solely because of abuse."[74] It is this latter attitude which has largely determined post-Reformation developments within Protestantism. At the same time the Reformers' search for the right middle way "chosen by Elizabeth" implies a *tertium datur* between a Mary-less Christianity and a superstitious Marian cult. Luther's angry call for abrogation of the Marian cult and the sharp criticism flowing out of the pen of Zwingli and Calvin should not be isolated but regarded as part of their quest for the right *via media*.

In a final section we should like to indicate some of the landmarks on this road that will have to be plotted on the ecclesiastical map of our time if we as *doctores* wish to discharge our responsibility for the Brethren, in the more restricted *and* in the larger sense of the word.

Natus ex Maria Virgine

1. The dangers on the right side of the *via media* are perhaps more conspicuous than those on the left: the Marian *leitourgia* has left marks on the *didache* which have become ineradicable in 1854, through the dogmatization of the Immaculate Conception, confirmed in 1950, by the promulgation of the dogma of the corporeal assumption of the Virgin Mary. Both dogmas show how far the tendency of drawing attention to the person rather than to the office of Mary has progressed.

73. "Atque hic cardo fidei Christianae versatur. ut credamus Christum filium dei in utero Virginis vere conceptum esse, absque tamen virili semine, virtute spiritus sancti," Zwingli, *SS.* VI. 204. Cf. Calvin, *CR* 45. 35.

74. "Ego velim, quod Mariae cultus penitus tollatur solum propter abusem." *WA* 11. 61.

The dogma of 1854, however, is the far more serious threat to a truly catholic Christology, because it isolates the mother of Christ from the rest of mankind by conferring upon her "such a fullness of innocence and sanctity, greater than which cannot be conceived under God."[75] Thus the radical depth of God's descent in the Incarnation is curtailed.

About the dogma of 1950 one can make the important positive observation that here a unity of body and soul is taught[76] which might give new, much needed life to the last words of the Apostolic Creed: "resurrection of the flesh." This applies, of course, only when Mary is seen as one of the faithful rather than as the mother of the Church who transcends the Church. Though proleptic, this presentation of the Virgin Mary can serve to show what God has in store for all the faithful, once his kingdom is fully established.

The lack of catholicity of this dogma is not so much due to its christological implications as to its significance for the relation of Scripture to Tradition and of these two to the *magisterium*. Never before has a doctrine been elevated to the status of dogma with so little support from either Scripture or the early Christian tradition. It has been carried and supported by strong waves of a Mariocentric piety which was in turn inspired by it. The great popularity of the *peregrinatio* of the Madonna of Fatima may lead to incidental criticisms on the part of progressive Roman Catholic theologians.[77] One may hope that evidence of the strength of the undercurrents of Marian piety

75. ". . . eam innocentiae et sanctitatis plenitudinem prae se ferret, qua maior sub Deo nullatenus intelligitur . . . ," in "Ineffabilis Deus," 8. XII. 1854; *Denz.* 2800. The observation by Jaroslav Pelikan is quite appropriate: "Not only must she be a warrant for the true humanity of Christ, her own true humanity must be recaptured," p. 142. René Laurentin points out that in the (medieval) debate about the Immaculate Conception, the Virgin Mary became for the first time "signe de contradiction." *La question mariale* (Paris, 1963), p. 60.

76. ". . . Corpore et anima ad supernam caeli gloriam eveheretur. . . ," in "Munificentissimus Deus." I. XI. 1950; *Denz.* 3902.

77. See the honest appraisal by Oskar Schroeder. "Die Diskussion über die wahre Marienverehrung in der römisch-katholischen Kirche von heute," *Eine heilige Kirche,* pp. 42–60. One reads with new interest his reference to two letters from the former Vice-Secretary of State Montini, the present Pope Paul VI. warning against sentimental Marian piety, p. 45. See also Pope John XXIII in *Osservatore Romano,* 25, XI. 1960.

shall force theologians to go beyond an Erasmian call for moderation.[78]

The intriguing interplay between Marian congresses and Mary-apparitions has led to the claim that this age should be regarded as the *epocha Mariana,* that the kingdom of Mary is the condition for the coming of the kingdom of Christ,[79] and finally that Mary should be regarded as *co-redemptrix,* argued on the basis of her *fiat* to cooperate in the Incarnation and her offer of Christ on the cross.[80]

Though one should acknowledge that the so-called maximalists form by no means a clear majority, the Protestant observer cannot help but be greatly concerned by the fact that the shift from the sources of Revelation to the *magisterium* frustrates any effort to bring the biblical witness to bear on Mariological developments within contemporary Roman Catholicism.[81]

The principle of development and growth has not yet been matched by a principle of reduction and trimming. Nevertheless, one should not conclude this section without pointing out that since the Pontificate of Pope John XXIII we have witnessed a series of unpredicted signs of renewal. For this reason it is more than ever appropriate to follow the example of Dr. G. C. Berkouwer who in 1948 kept open the avenue of hope

78. A most encouraging stance is taken by Bishop Paulus Rusch, who dares to go beyond any criticism known to me, when he says, for instance: "Unsere Glaübigen haben kein Christusgebet," in "Mariologische Wertungen," p. 134.

79. "Adveniat regnum Mariae, ut adveniat regnum Christi," Schroeder, p. 44.

80. An extremely clear and helpful survey of the present status of the theological discussion is *De natura co-redemptionis Marianae in theologia hodierna* (1921–1958), by Guilelmus Barauña (Rome, 1960), esp. pp. 105 ff. The Protestant theologian C. A. de Ridder stated in 1960 that though the number of those who reject the title "co-redemptrix" was decreasing, the time seemed not ripe for any official proclamation. *Maria Medeverlosseres?* (Utrecht, 1960), p. 123. This impression is confirmed by the discussion during the second session of Vatican II. See further Giovanni Miegge, *The Virgin Mary, the Roman Catholic Marian Doctrine* (London, 1955), esp. pp. 155 ff.

81. Cf. the statement by H. Volk, presently one of the leading progressive theologians: "Unser Glaube an die leibliche Aufnahme Mariens in den Himmel ist für uns völlig darin begrundet und rundum gesichert, dass die Kirche uns dies zu glauben lehrt." *Das neue Mariendogma* (Cologne, 1951), p. 25. See also my "Quo Vadis, Petre?" *Scottish Journal of Theology* 16 (1963), p. 253.

and expectation by terminating his discussion of Roman Catholic Mariology with the quotation from Luke 18:27: "What is impossible with men is possible with God."[82]

2. Malformations in Western Mariology are so much in evidence that one may well be inclined to echo the words of Luther: "I could wish that the cult of Mary would be completely abrogated, solely because of abuse." It might be a sign of a true ecumenical interpretation of the word "Brethren" if one would argue that the name of Mary has to be stricken out of Protestant thought and piety as an act of witness within the world Church, stemming not from a reactionary antipapalism but rather from a new emphasis on the positive original significance of the verb *protestari*.

One would, however, be unfaithful to the heritage of the Reformation if one were to interpret Protestantism solely as a "prophetic" critique accompanying the "priestly" Church. The Reformation tradition understands itself as the true manifestation and therefore continuation of the One, Holy, Catholic Church of the Apostolic Creed. Ecumenical theology does not presuppose and does not originate from a "seesaw" understanding of the Church, in the sense of the cold war "balance of power," but rather from the deeply felt need to grow in fullness of Truth, through "Lend-Lease" and through exposure to other traditions.

It is for this reason that Protestantism, not satisfied to function as the equalizer, searches to find the *via media,* to avoid not only Marian excesses at the right but also Marian minimalism at the left. The landmarks to the left of the *via media* are perhaps less prominent and eye-catching, but for that reason

---

82. *Conflict met Rome* (Kampen, 1948), p. 238. At the same time we should stress the relevance of Luther's rejection of the *fiducia*-in-Mary theme with which he was confronted. The last words of Pope John XXIII suggest to the Protestant observer that the attitude toward the Virgin Mary. described above in its late medieval context, is not a closed chapter in the history of Roman Catholic piety. At the solemn commemoration of the election of Pope John five years before on October 28, 1958, Cardinal L. Suenens of Brussels-Mechelen declared that the last barely audible words had been dedicated to the Virgin Mary when Pope John said: "My Mother, my confidence." *Katholiek Archief,* 18 (Dec., 1963), 50, col. 1286.

no less significant. Exactly in those traditions which one can characterize as minimalistic or even Mary-less, deep inroads have been made by the two main christological heresies: Docetism and Adoptionism. These heresies deny either that Jesus Christ is truly man or that he is truly God, and can therefore not accept the doctrine of the Incarnation as interpreted by the Council of Chalcedon (451) and signified by the Marian title *Theotokos*. In turn there is least interest in participating in the quest for the middle way in circles where the historical Jesus has been transformed into the Christ-idea or where Christ has become the teacher of great ethical truths.

3. As we saw in our discussion of the biblical image of the Virgin Mary, the virgin birth is located at the margin of the canon and cannot be regarded as part of the *kerygma*. It is a sign that this *kerygma* constitutes not only a message (Christ-idea) but also the beginning of a historical reality, *kaine ktisis,* the new creation. As a sign it requires interpretation and is open to misinterpretation, as the succeeding history has shown us. Acceptance of this sign cannot constitute a safeguard, guarantee, or doctrinal test for the true understanding of the mystery of the Incarnation.

At the same time, the biblical and classical Protestant appreciation of the functional significance of Mary is concisely expressed by Hans Asmussen, when he says: "One does not have Jesus Christ without Mary."[83] In this confession the true humanity of Christ is expressed. It would indeed be disregarding the biblical account of the *kerygma* and the historical evidence of the role the virginal birth played in the second-century doctrinal struggles if one were to make it a condition for orthodoxy to extend this statement to the *Virgin* Mary. However, in so far as "Virgin Mary" is a contraction and shorthand for the Chalcedonian "truly man and truly God," one will have to take the *natus ex maria virgine* seriously as the *didache* form in which the full meaning of the *kerygma* is perserved.

Though the very fact that Father Gustave Weigel could find

---

83. *Maria, die Mutter Gottes* (Stuttgart, 1950), p. 137.

traces of Nestorianism in Paul Tillich[84] while Father George Tavard noted "an unavowed Docetism"[85] in him could suggest the proximity of this great theologian to Chalcedonian orthodoxy, one cannot help but be disconcerted by his observation that just as "Apollo has no revelatory significance for Christians: the Virgin Mother Mary reveals nothing to Protestants."[86]

The same observations we have made with reference to the virginal birth could be applied to the *Theotokos* title. When it is interpreted to mean that the child of Mary is the eternal Son of God, its rejection implies the denial of the biblical understanding of the Incarnation. At the same time we have seen that Nestorius's objection to the use of this title might well have stemmed from his concern about Mariological aberrations connected with it. History provided ample proof that this title could become the justification for a further entrenchment of a physical-metaphysical "womb" theology clearly rejected by Jesus. It is the task of the Protestant theologian to be the sentry protecting the right understanding of the *Theotokos* title, alerted whenever this title is rejected, aware that its use is no guarantee for orthodoxy,[87] acknowledging it as a *didachean* form in which the *kerygma* is preserved and transmitted.[88]

4. Our discussion of the virgin birth and the *Theotokos* title did not contain a hidden plea for the development of a Mariology on Protestant soil. It rather suggests that an independent Mariology cannot do justice to the biblical presentation

---

84. "Contemporaneous Protestantism and Paul Tillich," *Theological Studies* 8 (1950), p. 194.

85. *Paul Tillich and the Christian Message* (New York, 1961), p. 131.

86. *Systematic Theology* I (Chicago, 1951), p. 128.

87. Michael Servetus does not hesitate to use *Theotokos* or *Dei Genetrix* to designate the Virgin Mary; see George H. Williams, *The Radical Reformation* (Philadelphia, 1962), pp. 326, 337. Caspar Schwenckfeld can reconcile his "celestial flesh" concept of Christ's human nature with the *Theotokos* title. See Paul L. Maier, *Caspar Schwenckfeld on the Person and Work of Christ* (Assen, 1959), pp. 55 ff., p. 61.

88. Cf. Karl Barth: "Die Abwehr des Missbrauchs, der mit der in dieser Bezeichnung ausgesprochenen Erkenntnis getrieben worden ist, wird nicht fehlen dürfen. Aber jene Erkenntnis und darum auch diese Bezeichnung selbst darf deswegen doch nicht unterdrückt werden." I. 2, p. 152.

of the figure of Mary, the mother of Jesus Christ. What we have called "womb" theology proved to be the reliable indication that the Virgin Mary was being hypostatized and granted a place in her own right alongside or even opposite Christ. Our conclusion has to be that a truly catholic and evangelical Mariology is Christology.

This is not an arithmetical equation and therefore not arithmetically reversible, since Jesus Christ is not only *natus ex maria virgine,* but also and first *conceptus a spiritu sancto.* There is more to be said about Jesus Christ than we can glean from the figure of Mary, and because of this "more" it is important and worthwhile to say anything at all. But this kerygmatic "more" cannot be expressed, preserved, and transmitted when one bypasses the figure of Mary; her office is that of a beacon which one cannot ignore without peril. She is chosen into this office, *mutatis mutandis,* just as "the First Lady" is chosen into office as the President's wife. "Virgin" and *Theotokos* can then be looked upon as degrees conferred upon her, *honoris causa,* to express respect for the Presidential office rather than for her personal qualities. This is what Luther had in mind when he hailed the Virgin Mary as *fabrica,* the workshop of God, and what Calvin formulated when he called her blessed as the elect instrument of God's work of redemption.

Thus, we may be enabled to find the *via media* in the Church of our time, aware of the dangers for Christology in a Mary-less Christianity on the one side, and a Marian personality cult on the other side. When speaking in responsibility to the Brethren in a wider sense of the word, i.e., to the *fratres separati,* we shall have to emphasize this latter danger as strongly as at the time of the Reformation; when speaking in responsibility to our more closely related Brethren, we might today have to emphasize the former even more than in the sixteenth century.

Lex credendi est lex orandi

In a few words we now indicate some of the subsidiary offices which are not to the same extent unique to the Virgin Mary, but exactly for that reason are possibly beacons for the Church of our time in areas where vision seems jeopardized.

With the expression "subsidiary offices" we wish to indicate that the proper understanding of the place and role of the Virgin Mary in the life of the Church is not restricted to Christology but has of necessity its impact on other areas as well, not the least of which is the worship of the Church. This is indeed the appropriate direction, but formulated by inversion of the traditional adage: *lex credendi est lex orandi.*

1. Together with Simeon, Anna, Zachariah, Elizabeth and John the Baptist, Mary belongs to the expecting Church on the threshold of fulfillment between the Old and the New Covenant. Confronted with the phenomenon of a culturalized American Protestantism, which tends to become a New Testament Christianity, it may be not without significance to be alerted to the historical continuity of the Church as the people of God. In order to see the full dimensions of the kingship of Christ, it is important to retrace this history beyond Pentecost to Abraham, the father of all believers.

2. From an unexpected side—the great liberal historian of Christian thought, Adolf von Harnack—we are reminded that there are truly evangelical elements in the medieval understanding of the place of the Virgin Mary vis-à-vis God.[89] Indeed, provided she is seen as the *typus ecclesiae,* i.e., as the prototype of the faithful, there is great soteriological relevance in her bold dealings with God, in which one can find a proper understanding of Hebrews 4:16: "Let us then with confidence draw near to the throne of grace, that we may receive mercy and find grace to help in time of need."

3. From an evangelical perspective it is clear that the role of the Virgin Mary within the context of the Christian *leitourgia* cannot be to receive our prayers in order that she

89. "Das einzig Versöhnende an der Mariologie is die Wahrnehmung, dass der fromme Glaube sich über das Verhältnis der Maria zu Gott und Christus Aussagen erlaubt, die er über sein eigenes Verhältnis nicht zu machen wagt. In diesem Sinn ist in der Marienlehre—es scheint freilich paradox—manches Evangelische." *Lehrbuch der Dogmengeschichte* III (Tübingen, 1932), p. 655, n. 1.

may intercede for us with God. She is not to be looked upon as the "mother of mercy," *mater misericordiae,* over against the Son or the Father as the severe judge.

But when the Church is taken seriously as a fellowship of memory and hope, the *koinonia* is extended through space *and* time. The dimensions of Christian worship are enlarged when the militant Church does not isolate itself as an ever-repeated new beginning, but exercises the fellowship spanning the times by praying not *to,* but *with* those who have gone before.

On October 11, 1963, Pope Paul VI said in a prayer concluding his speech in S. Maria Maggiore that with the Western separated Brethren "the remembrance and the veneration for you, O Mary, begins to dawn like morning. Call with us all these your sons to the same unity under your maternal and celestial protection."[90]

At the end of our investigation we have reason to wonder whether it is either appropriate or realistic to invoke the protection of the Virgin Mary for the rapproachement to which an ever-increasing number of Christians of both confessions are dedicating themselves today.[91] When, however, we are allowed to interpret her call to unity as the light of the beacon pointing away from herself to Jesus Christ, Protestants and Roman Catholics can join in hailing her as "the mother of God."

90. Published by Ufficio Stampa, Concilio Ecumenico Vaticano II, Handreich-ungen in Deutscher Sprache Nr. 27, 16. X. 63. Cf. Pope Leo XIII: ". . . permagnum unitatis christianae praesidium divinitus oblatum est in Maria." Litt. enc. *Adiutricem populi,* in *Leonis XIII Acta* XV. 308. Quoted by Carolus Balic, "De motu mariologico-mariano et motione oecumenica XIX et XX," *De mariologia et oecumenismo,* p. 528.

91. René Laurentin, among Mariologists the most aware of Protestant life and thought, rightly warns against the tendency to find in contemporary Protestantism "symptomes de redécouverte de la Vierge." *La question mariale,* p. 132. The rule which he indicates as the guideline for his own task can be accepted also by a Protestant as a realistic *and* promising ecumenical program for the years ahead: "Redécouvrir la Vierge *dans* la Bible, tandis que les Protestants la decouvriraient *par* la Bible." Ibid., p. 141.

For Further Reading

ASMUSSEN, H. *Maria die Mutter Gottes.* Stuttgart: Evangelisches Verlagswerk, 1951.

BENKO, STEPHEN. *Protestants, Catholics, and Mary.* Valley Forge: Judson Press, 1968.

BOSLOOPER, T. *The Virgin Birth.* Philadelphia: Westminster, 1962.

DELIUS, W. "Luther und die Marienverehrung." *Theologische Literaturzietung* 79 (1954): 409–14.

DUPUY, B. D., O. P. "La Mariologie de Calvin." *Istina* 5 (1958): 479–92.

EBNETER, A. "Martin Luthers Marienbild." *Orientierung* 20 (1956): 77–79, 85–87.

FEDERER, K. "Zwingli und die Marienverehrung." *Zeitschrift für Schweizer Kirchengeschichte* 45 (1951): 17–21.

FRIETHOFF, C. S. J. M., O. P. *A Complete Mariology.* Westminster: Newman, 1958.

HÂMER, J., O. P. "Protestants and the Marian Doctrine." *The Thomist* 17 (1955): 480–502.

LAURENTIN, R. *Court traité de théologie mariale.* Paris: Lethielleux, 1953.

LOCHER, G. W. "Inhalt und Absicht von Zwinglis Marienlehre." *Kirchenblatt für die reformierte Schweiz* 107 (1951): 34–37.

O'MEARA, THOMAS, O. P. *Mary in Protestant and Catholic Theology.* New York: Sheed & Ward, 1966.

PITTENGER, N. "The Devotion to the Mother of Christ in Catholic Spirituality." *Anglican Theological Review* 31 (1951): 71–81.

PREUSS, H. D. "Maria bei Luther." Schriften des Vereins für Reformationsgeschichte, Vol. 172. Gütersloh: Gerd Mohn, 1954.

TAIT, L. GORDON. "Karl Barth and the Virgin Mary." *Journal of Ecumenical Studies* 4 (1967): 406–25.

THURIAN, M. "Le dogme de l'Assomption." *Verbum Caro* 5 (1951).

Facet Books Already Published

16. *Introduction to Pharisaism*
    by W. D. Davies. 1967
17. *Man and Nature in the New Testament*
    by C. F. D. Moule. 1967
18. *The Lord's Supper According to the New Testament*
    by Eduard Schweizer (translated by James M. Davis). 1967
19. *The Psalms: A Form-Critical Introduction*
    by Hermann Gunkel (translated by Thomas M. Horner). 1967
20. *The Spirit-Paraclete in the Fourth Gospel*
    by Hans Windisch (translated by James W. Cox). 1968
21. *The Semitic Background of the Term "Mystery" in the New Testament*
    by Raymond E. Brown, S.S. 1968
22. *The Beginnings of Christology: A Study in Its Problems*
    by Willi Marxsen (translated by Paul J. Achtemeier). 1969
23. *The Theology of The Book of Ruth*
    by Ronald M. Hals. 1969
24. *Luke the Historian in Recent Study*
    by C. K. Barrett. 1970
25. *The Lord's Supper as a Christological Problem*
    by Willi Marxsen (translated by Lorenz Nieting). 1970
26. *The "I Am" of the Fourth Gospel*
    by Philip B. Harner. 1970
27. *The Gospels and Contemporary Biographies in the Greco-Roman World*
    by Clyde Weber Votaw. 1970
28. *Was Jesus a Revolutionist?* by Martin Hengel
    (translated by William Klassen). 1971
29. *Iscariot* by Bertil Gärtner
    (translated by Victor I. Gruhn). 1971

Social Ethics Series:

1. *Our Calling*
   by Einar Billing (translated by Conrad Bergendoff). 1965
2. *The World Situation*
   by Paul Tillich. 1965
3. *Politics as a Vocation*
   by Max Weber (translated by H. H. Gerth and C. Wright Mills). 1965
4. *Christianity in a Divided Europe*
   by Hanns Lilje. 1965
5. *The Bible and Social Ethics*
   by Hendrik Kraemer. 1965

6. *Christ and the New Humanity*
   by C. H. Dodd. 1965
7. *What Christians Stand For in the Secular World*
   by William Temple. 1965
8. *Legal Responsibility and Moral Responsibility*
   by Walter Moberly. 1965
9. *The Divine Command: A New Perspective on Law and Gospel*
   by Paul Althaus (translated by Franklin Sherman). 1966
10. *The Road to Peace*
    by John C. Bennett, Kenneth Johnstone, C. F. von Weizsäcker, Michael Wright. 1966
11. *The Idea of a Natural Order: With an Essay on Modern Asceticism*
    by V. A. Demant. 1966
12. *Kerygma, Eschatology, and Social Ethics*
    by Amos N. Wilder. 1966
13. *Affluence and the Christian*
    by Hendrik van Oyen (translated by Frank Clarke). 1966
14. *Luther's Doctrine of the Two Kingdoms*
    by Heinrich Bornkamm (translated by Karl H. Hertz). 1966
15. *Christian Decision in the Nuclear Age*
    by T. R. Milford. 1967
16. *Law and Gospel*
    by Werner Elert (translated by Edward H. Schroeder). 1967
17. *On Marriage*
    by Karl Barth (translated by A. T. Mackay *et al.*). 1968